TRUST ME MY BELOVED

Copyright © 2021 Ciara Mason Trust Me My Beloved

All rights reserved. No part of this publication may be reproduced, distributed, or transmitted in any form or by any means, including photocopying, recording, or other electronic or mechanical methods, without the prior written permission of the publisher, except in the case of brief quotations embodied in critical reviews and certain other noncommercial uses permitted by copyright law. For permission requests, write to the publisher, addressed "Attention: Permissions Coordinator," at the address below.

Contribution by Kiyanni Bryan, Write It Out Publishing LLC in the United States of America.

Illustrator: Maurice Rogers
Editor: Tamira K. Butler-Likely
Intext Design: Jason Josiah

ISBN: 978-1-7371761-5-2 (Paperback)
First Printing, 2021

Ciara Mason
Suffolk VA 23435
info@ciaramason.com
www.ciaramason.com

TRUST ME MY BELOVED

Written by
Ciara Mason

Write It Out Publishing LLC.

Dedication

I dedicate this book to my husband, who is my strength, my three princesses, who are my why, my parents, who are my stabilizers, and to the Razing Women who pushed me to TRUST God for myself.

Table of Contents

Dedication iv
Introduction 1
God the Creator 4
God the Comedian 8
God the Promise Keeper 12
God the Provider 16
God the Friend 20
God the Name Changer 24
God That Is With You 28
God the Qualifier 32
God the Thrifter 36
God the Coach 40
God the Deliverer 44
God the Miracle Worker 48
God Our Banner 52
God the Jealous God 56
God Who Rewards the Fearless 60
God the Defender 64
God the Cycle Breaker 67
God of the Encore 71
God the Strategist 75
God of the Impossible 79
God Our Peace 83
God the Restorer 87
God the Void Filler 90
The God Who Rewards Sacrifice 94

The God Who Favors 98
God That Gives Beauty for Ashes 102
The God That Remembers 106
The God That Reveals the Future 109
God Our Strength............................. 113
God is Love....................................... 118

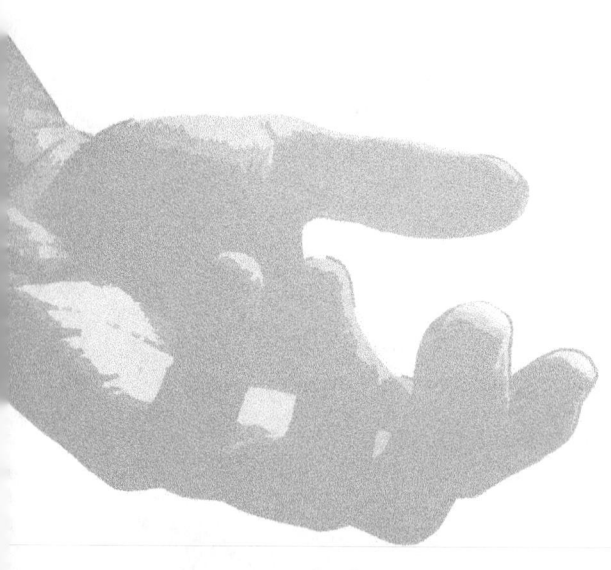

Introduction

Hey there, God's beloved,

I am so excited that you chose to join in on this journey towards complete trust in the Father. If you are reading this letter, know that this is not a coincidence. More than likely, you have been longing to grow closer to God and mature in your walk with Him. Don't get me wrong, you know Him, but there's a burning desire within you to know Him more intimately. You're in the right place. I am fully confident that this devotional will prove to be one of the keys to your victory.

In my personal journey with the Lord, I have found that it wasn't necessarily the Sunday morning sermons that anchored my trust in God, but it was the daily pursuit and private seeking that drew me closer to Him. The more I read His word, the more I came to know Him. The more I came to know Him, the easier it was for me to trust Him. The more my trust grew, the less I feared and worried. It's such a beautiful domino effect. May this become your testimony as well.

Over the next 30 days, you will hear the Father speaking directly to your heart, reintroducing you to His unchanging characteristics. While this is not an exhaustive view of Him, it's certainly a good start! My prayer is that by the end of this journey you will be able to say you truly trust God, not based on what you've heard, but on what you know about your Father.

One more thing before we dive in. You will notice that at the end of each day, there are questions, or what I like to call writing prompts. Take time to truly ponder and answer these questions as they will help you to identify roots, opened doors and areas of life that could benefit from more of your attention and prayer.

Are you ready for the journey? I know you are! Take a moment now to set a time to meet the Father daily with your Bible, this devotional, a journal, and a soft worship instrumental (if that's your thing). The Father's hand is extended, take the step! Let the journey to trust begin!

In Perfect Love,

Ciara Mason

"Those who know your name trust in you, for you, O Lord, do not abandon those who search for you."

Psalm 9:10 (NLT)

Day 1

God the Creator

1 In the beginning God created the heavens and the earth. 31 God saw all that he had made, and it was very good. And there was evening, and there was morning—the sixth day.
- Genesis 1:1,31 (NIV)

What better way to start your journey towards getting to know me, your father, in a more intimate way than by recognizing me as creator. The first revelation that I desire for you to have of me is that I am the creator. Notice that I didn't say I am "a" creator or someone who simply creates, I AM THE Creator. John 1:3 informs you that through me all things were made; without me nothing was made that has been made. I brought to life all things, including you. You are my most prized creation. If you need to be reminded, take a moment to read Psalm 139:13-16.

    Do you see the amount of detail that I put into creating you? I graciously knit you together. Have you ever seen someone knit or weave? This takes time, planning, patience, and love. I was intentional when I made you. I gave you specific features, characteristics, and intricacies. I fully stocked you with everything you would need to fulfill the plan I wrote out for your life before you even came to be. You are wonderfully made. YOU ARE NOT A MISTAKE! You were created with

purpose, on purpose. So live proud of who you are and rejoice in me, your masterful creator.

Whisper This Prayer!

God, thank you for taking time to hand knit me in my mother's womb. I acknowledge that all you created, including me, you called good. You did not make any mistakes when you created me. You formed me in my mother's womb with purpose, with gifts, with destiny, and with an established end. Help me to embrace who you created me to be and to honor your craftsmanship. I release you to continue to create a beautiful masterpiece out of our lives. In Jesus' name, Amen.

What aspects of yourself have you had a hard time seeing as good?

God hasn't stopped creating, what do you need Him to create in your life, today?

_____
_____
_____
_____
_____
_____
_____
_____
_____
_____
_____
_____
_____

"God created everything through him, and nothing was created except through him."

John 1:3 (NLT)

DAY 2

God the Comedian

12 So she laughed silently to herself and said, "How could a worn-out woman like me enjoy such pleasure, especially when my master—my husband—is also so old?"
Genesis 18:12 (NLT)

This characteristic is one that you may not be acquainted with just yet. However, I assure you that as you continue to walk with me, you too will experience the laughter that only I can provoke. I AM He who does the impossible, in my perfect timing. I don't forget my promises, even when you've given up hope for them. Just as I made Sarah laugh when I sent word that even at an old age she would give birth to a promise, you too shall laugh at the things I do on your behalf, at the ordained moment. Prepare your heart now to laugh, in awe, not in doubt. You shall laugh with your friends with tears in your eyes, declaring, "God really did it for me."

Whisper This Prayer!

God, thank you for your perfect plan for my life. Even though everything hasn't happened the way I felt it should or at the time I thought it would, I still believe you. Help me to fully trust your timing for every good thing in my life. Help me to grow in faith and not in doubt as I await the manifestation of what you have promised. Time doesn't rob you of power. I know that full well. Remind me of this truth when my faith has grown weary. I trust you, please teach me to trust you more. In Jesus' name, Amen.

"God is not a man, so he does not lie. He is not human, so he does not change his mind. Has he ever spoken and failed to act?"

Numbers 23:19 (NLT)

What promises are you hearing from the Father, even at this moment, that you're having trouble believing?

Have you allowed the disappointment of seemingly overlooked prayers or delayed answers to taint your trust?

_____
_____
_____
_____
_____
_____
_____
_____
_____
_____
_____
_____

"God is not a man, so he does not lie. He is not human, so he does not change his mind. Has he ever spoken and failed to act?"

Numbers 23:19 (NLT)

DAY 3

God the Promise Keeper

> *1The Lord kept his word and did for Sarah exactly what he had promised. 6 And Sarah declared, "God has brought me laughter. All who hear about this will laugh with me…"*
> **Genesis 21:1,6 (NLT)**

I've said it once but I will say it until you believe me. I AM the God who doesn't forget His promises, even when you've given up hope for them. I need you to trust me to not break a promise or your heart. The powerful thing about being in relationship with me is that if I say a thing, it has to be. Remember, my words create. So once I make a decree out of the heavens, every atom and molecule in Earth begins to move and collide in order to make what I said manifest. It's safe to say, I can't lie! If I make you a promise, I can't renege on it. I know the length of time between promise and performance can cause you to doubt that I'll show up, but fight to patiently wait, with expectation, for me to fulfill my promises. I can and I will!

Whisper This Prayer!

God, thank you for being a promise-keeping God. I am grateful that you are not like man, in that you cannot lie. I ask you, Lord, to help me to take you at your word. To believe that you are able to do that which you have promised me. No matter how long it takes, help me not to waiver in my belief that YOU CAN. Help me to remember that your timing is always perfect. I trust you, please teach me to trust you more. In Jesus' name, Amen.

Are there any promises of God that you have completely lost faith in or given up on?

_____

_____

_____

_____

_____

_____

_____

_____

_____

_____

_____

_____

_____

_____

_____

_____

_____

_____

_____

_____

Take a moment to remind yourself of the promises that have not yet manifested in your life. Don't get upset! Write them down. Commit to praying these promises through and regain your expectation for their fulfillment.

_____
_____
_____
_____
_____
_____
_____
_____
_____

"Not a single one of all the good promises the Lord had given to the family of Israel was left unfulfilled; everything he had spoken came true."

Joshua 21:45 (NLT)

DAY 4

God the Provider

13 Then Abraham looked up and saw a ram caught by its horns in a thicket. So he took the ram and sacrificed it as a burnt offering in place of his son. 14 Abraham named the place Yahweh-Yireh (which means "the Lord will provide"). To this day, people still use that name as a proverb: "On the mountain of the Lord it will be provided."
Genesis 22:13-14 (NLT)

When you hear the word provision, nine times out of ten, your mind goes to finances. While I am the supplier of your financial needs, please remember that I have so much more to offer. Every day I provide you with peace, joy, love, wisdom, guidance, a way of escape, strength… the list goes on. Anything that you could ever need or even desire, I have, in abundance.

 Remember my servant Abraham, who in obedience to my voice was willing to offer up his precious son as a sacrifice. Being that I wasn't after his son but after his devotion and faith, I stopped his planned sacrifice and provided him with an alternative sacrifice, a ram. In the same way, over 2,000 years ago, I saw your need for a savior. I knew that according to the law, you would need a sacrifice for the sins you would surely commit. Seeing the need and desiring to be one with you, I sent my only begotten son

Jesus to be the alternative sacrifice for your life. This is the ultimate display of provision. If I was willing to give my son for the sins of the world, what could you ever ask for that I can't provide?

Whisper This Prayer!

God, thank you for your consistent provision for me. Everything I have ever needed your hands have provided, and for that I am grateful. I thank you today, especially for the provision of salvation you have made available to me through the finished work and shed blood of Christ at Calvary. I recognize that if you would give your son for me to have life, there's no need that you will leave unfulfilled. Teach me how to fully rely on you without fear or doubt. You have not failed me and you won't start now. In Jesus' name, Amen.

Can you recall a time when you needed God most and He came through with the provision you needed? Write about it.

_____
_____
_____
_____
_____
_____
_____

While God may have scared you once or twice when it comes to provision, has He ever failed you?

_____
_____
_____
_____
_____
_____
_____

What do you need God to provide MOST in your life right now? Can you bring your heart to believe that He Can and He will provide?

_____

_____

_____

_____

_____

_____

_____

_____

_____

_____

_____

> "And this same God who takes care of me will supply all your needs from his glorious riches, which have been given to us in Christ Jesus."
>
> Philippians 4:19 (NLT)

Day 5

God the Friend

> 17 The LORD said, "Shall I keep secret from Abraham [My friend and servant] what I am going to do…"
> **Genesis 18:17 (AMP)**

Friends, how many of you have them? Friends, ones you can depend on. For many of you, friendship has proven to be a hard thing to sustain. You meet people and you just know you're going to be life-long friends. Unfortunately, as time progresses, you find that they are manipulative, or self-seeking and you're left hurting and angry. What a disappointment!

Today, I've sent you this little folded up note, with one question and two empty boxes inside. "Will you be my best friend? Yes, or No?" I long to be friends with you, as I was with Abraham. I desire closeness with you so that I can confide in you as you confide in me. I want someone I can share my secrets with. I'm looking for someone who will come into my presence and sit with me without asking for a thing. I have so many associates, those who know me only through someone else. I'm looking for a friend and I'd love for it to be you!

Whisper This Prayer!

God, thank you for giving me the privilege of being called your friend. It is an honor to walk through life with you beside me. My desire is to be one that you can trust with your heart and your secrets. Teach me how to be intentional about spending time with you and getting to know you better. In Jesus' name, Amen.

What do you consider to be necessary qualities of a friend?

_____
_____
_____
_____
_____
_____
_____
_____

Based on the qualities listed above, would you say you are a friend of God or an associate?

_____
_____
_____
_____
_____
_____
_____
_____
_____
_____

What actions can you take to make yourself a (better) friend to God?

_____
_____
_____
_____
_____
_____
_____
_____
_____
_____
_____
_____
_____

"And so it happened just as the Scriptures say: "Abraham believed God, and God counted him as righteous because of his faith." He was even called the friend of God."

James 2:23 (NLT)

DAY 6

God the Name Changer

27 "What is your name?" the man asked. He replied, "Jacob." 28 "Your name will no longer be Jacob," the man told him. "From now on you will be called Israel, because you have fought with God and with men and have won."
Genesis 32:27-28 (NLT)

Everyone has a past, old ways and old names. I am fully aware that you were born in sin and shaped in iniquity. However, through the finished work of my son, Jesus, you have the opportunity to walk free from your past. Because of Jesus' sacrifice on Calvary, you are able to confess your faults to me and have your entire history erased. Regardless of what your past includes, we can rest assured that I AM more than able to change your name.

    Remember my servant Jacob, whose birth name meant supplanter, someone or something that wrongfully takes the place of another. If I could put it in terms you can relate to, Jacob's name meant trickster, a con artist, or a fraud, and he was living up to his name. However, Jacob grew close to me and had a relentless pursuit of my blessing (seal of approval). He wrestled until his old nature died. I marked his fresh start with a name change. No longer was he to be identified by his old nature (trickster), but he was to now be acknowledged as Israel, meaning prince of God. The same can and will be done for you. Keep wrestling with my word, keep pursuing me, and watch your old ways and name melt like wax.

Whisper This Prayer!

God, thank you for loving me enough to change my name. Thank you for seeing beyond my past and calling me into my true identity in you. Today I commit to leaving my old name and ways behind and fully embracing my new identity in you. I am NOT who I used to be. There has been a change in my life and I refuse to go back. Strengthen me in my moments of weakness. Surround me with people who will see the best in me and hold me accountable to this new life in you. I trust you to be my keeper. In Jesus' name, Amen.

What names are you answering to today or have answered to in the past that don't match what God says about you (i.e., lonely, worthless, stupid, fast, wimp, etc.)?

_____
_____
_____
_____
_____
_____
_____

Do you believe that God, by His power, is able to not only change your name but to change your nature?

_____
_____
_____
_____
_____
_____
_____

What steps are you taking (or plan to take) to ensure you never return to your old name again?

_____
_____
_____
_____
_____
_____
_____
_____
_____
_____

"What's more, I am changing your name. It will no longer be Abram. Instead, you will be called Abraham, for you will be the father of many nations."

Genesis 17:5 (NLT)

DAY 7

God That Is With You

2The Lord was with Joseph, so he succeeded in everything he did as he served in the home of his Egyptian master. 3 Potiphar noticed this and realized that the Lord was with Joseph, giving him success in everything he did.
Genesis 39:2-3 (NLT)

Be confident of this fact, my beloved, wherever you find yourself today, I am there with you. I AM the omnipresent God, able to be everywhere at the same time. As I spoke in Psalm 139, if you go up to the heavens, I AM there; if you make your bed in hell, I AM there. If you rise on the wings of the dawn, if you settle on the far side of the sea, even there, my hand will guide you and my right hand will hold you fast.

    Remember my servant Joseph and his journey through jealousy and hatred from family, being sold into slavery, false accusations from his master's wife, and a jail sentence. While his life's story is riddled with hardship, I want you to intentionally look for my Glory shining in his darkest moments. I was with him, every step of the journey. I allowed his gifts to be utilized in every setting he stepped into. I favored his life and caused all of his superiors to trust him and promote him. Joseph's life is proof that all things really do work together for the good of those who love me. So, I encourage you, whether you find yourself in a pit, a palace, or a prison, know that I AM right beside you, grooming you, and waiting for the perfect opportunity to cause you to shine! It's all working together for your GOOD!

Whisper This Prayer!

God, thank you for your consistent presence in my life. I recognize that through all of life's trials you have never forsaken me. You have caused everything to work together for my good. Help me to trust you, even when I can't see you. Help me to know that even in the midst of darkness you are with me. You know what's best for me. I trust you with my life. In Jesus' name, Amen.

Take a moment to look back over your life. Think of the toughest moment you've had to encounter (emotions are okay, let it happen). Now, in the middle of the darkness, LOOK FOR GOD. Write down how God proved to be with you even in your darkest moment.

_____
_____
_____
_____
_____
_____
_____
_____
_____
_____
_____
_____
_____
_____
_____
_____
_____

How much different would the outcome of that event be if God were NOT present?

_____

_____

_____

_____

_____

_____

_____

_____

_____

_____

_____

> "And we know that God causes everything to work together for the good of those who love God and are called according to his purpose for them."
> Romans 8:28 (NLT)

DAY 8

God the Qualifier

12 God answered, "I will be with you. And this is your sign that I am the one who has sent you: When you have brought the people out of Egypt, you will worship God at this very mountain." 13 But Moses protested, "If I go to the people of Israel and tell them, 'The God of your ancestors has sent me to you,' they will ask me, 'What is his name?' Then what should I tell them?" 14 God replied to Moses, "I AM WHO I AM. Say this to the people of Israel: I AM has sent me to you."

Exodus 3:12-14 (NLT)

As you move deeper into this relationship of trust in me, I want to remind you that it is I that qualifies you. I've heard your cry to be used for my Glory. I see your heart's desire to truly please me with your obedience to my voice. You asked to be sent, so I whispered marching orders in your ear. "Here is where I need you the most, my beloved. Go!" I whispered. Almost instantly, our beautiful moment of total surrender was overtaken by your doubts and excuses.

Before you could even dry your eyes you had already made a list of 10 reasons why you aren't QUALIFIED to complete the assignment. "But God, I'm not smart enough to do that. I don't have enough money to start that. I don't have enough support, no one knows me..." your list grew on and on, breaking my heart. Is my spirit living within you not enough? Do you think I'd push you out into purpose just to leave you? Never! So here I am again, bringing the assignment back to you with a little note on top that simply says, YOU'RE QUALIFIED FOR THIS. Go!

Whisper This Prayer!

God, thank you for seeing more in me than I often see in myself. Thank you for calling me and choosing me to carry out your will in the Earth. Today, Father, I repent for every 'no,' 'not now,' and 'I can't' that I gave you in response to your call. Forgive me for being selfish and considering only my comfort and security. I ask that you endow me with strength to give you a real, 'Yes.' I no longer desire to live a life of complacency. I want to be used by you. I want to make you proud. I trust you with my life. In Jesus' name, Amen.

What assignment(s) from God have you failed to follow through on?

What are your reasons for denying or delaying your obedience?

_____
_____
_____
_____
_____
_____
_____
_____
_____
_____

Just for Thought: How many people are suffering or going without because of your lack of submission?

"God will make this happen, for he who calls you is faithful."

1 Thessalonians 5:24 (NLT)

DAY 9

God the Thrifter

2 Then the Lord asked him, "What is that in your hand?" "A shepherd's staff," Moses replied. 3 "Throw it down on the ground," the Lord told him. So Moses threw down the staff, and it turned into a snake! Moses jumped back. 4 Then the Lord told him, "Reach out and grab its tail." So Moses reached out and grabbed it, and it turned back into a shepherd's staff in his hand. 5 "Perform this sign," the Lord told him. "Then they will believe that the Lord, the God of their ancestors—the God of Abraham, the God of Isaac, and the God of Jacob—really has appeared to you."
Exodus 4:2-5 (NLT)

Based on the culture you grew up in, the word thrifter may have a negative connotation, so allow me to explain what I mean when I say I'm the ultimate thrifter. A thrifter is a person who finds pleasure in rummaging through old items that others have deemed outdated, holding little value, or even trash, and seeing treasure. I take great joy in taking what the world has discarded and repurposing it. People, abilities, things, places, you name it and I can show you the value and purpose in it.

Remember my servant Moses and what he had in his hand when we met. He saw it as a shepherd's staff, I saw it as an instrument of power to make my presence undeniable. I wish to do the same with what you hold in your hands, heart, and mind. So I ask you, what is that in your hand, beloved? Is that a witty idea, a song, a passion, a hurt, or a talent you are holding but not putting to use? Submit it to me today. Throw it down at my feet and allow me to show you the power of it. What you saw as useless yesterday, I present to you today as priceless.

Whisper This Prayer!

God, thank you for first seeing value and purpose in me. Thank you for taking me in as your prized possession when everyone else cast me away. I ask that today you will show me what's in my hands. Show me the ability, the gift, the knowledge, that's lying within me waiting to be used as a symbol of your power and presence. As I identify my own personal "staff," help me, Father, to see its value. Use every aspect of my life to display your power, Lord, I surrender. In Jesus' name, Amen.

What do you have in your 'hand'? What aspect of your life have you underestimated or failed to see the value in?

_____
_____
_____
_____
_____
_____
_____
_____
_____
_____

Considering all that you have, how can you put these things into use starting today? (Example, you may have a love for helping hurting people. Allow that love to drive you to the nearest shelter to volunteer or to the nearest corner to gift someone with a meal.)

_____
_____
_____
_____

"We now have this light shining in our hearts, but we ourselves are like fragile clay jars containing this great treasure. This makes it clear that our great power is from God, not from ourselves."

2 Corinthians 4:7 (NLT)

Day 10

God the Coach

10 But Moses pleaded with the Lord, "O Lord, I'm not very good with words. I never have been, and I'm not now, even though you have spoken to me. I get tongue-tied, and my words get tangled." 11 Then the Lord asked Moses, "Who makes a person's mouth? Who decides whether people speak or do not speak, hear or do not hear, see or do not see? Is it not I, the Lord? 12 Now go! I will be with you as you speak, and I will instruct you in what to say."
Exodus 4:10-12 (NLT)

Journey back in time with me. You're back in your high school gymnasium on a Friday night. It's basketball season. You're dressed in your team uniform, sneakers laced up, water bottle in hand, sitting on the bench cheering your teammates on. The referee's whistle blows. "Time out," he yells. You lift up the bottle to take another sip of your water, when suddenly you hear the coach shout your name. "You're in," he yells, motioning for you to go out on the court. "No," you yell back. "Please choose someone else." Confused, the coach rushes to you seated on the bench. "Why would I choose someone else when I chose you? I picked you for this team for this exact moment. Only you can run the secret play we've been practicing. We need you, we believe in you," the coach gently whispers with his hand on your shoulder. Now you sit, having to make a decision.

Do you run out on the court and run the play that will ensure victory for not just yourself but for the entire team? Or do you remain seated comfortably on the bench, pretending to not have heard the call? Today, I beg you to GO! Now is the time. You've prepared for this moment. I've called you. There are no replacements. The victory of the team depends greatly on your "yes." We need you. We believe in you! Now GO!

Whisper This Prayer!

God, thank you for giving me another chance to hear your call and to respond in faith. Thank you for choosing me out of all of the people in the world to carry out this beautiful assignment. I can no longer pretend and hide. I hear you calling me, and today I respond with a "Yes." Thank you again for hand picking me. I love and trust you. In Jesus' name, Amen.

What's keeping you tied to the "bench" today? You now know you're qualified and you have all you need within you. What are you allowing to hold you back?

_____
_____
_____
_____
_____
_____
_____
_____
_____
_____
_____
_____
_____
_____
_____
_____
_____
_____
_____

Of the things you listed, which of these is stronger than your God? If you're having a hard time answering this question, instead write down all the reasons why you must leave the bench.

_____

_____

_____

_____

_____

_____

_____

_____

_____

> "You didn't choose me. I chose you. I appointed you to go and produce lasting fruit, so that the Father will give you whatever you ask for, using my name."
>
> John 15:16 (NLT)

Day 11

God the Deliverer

6 "Therefore, say to the people of Israel: 'I am the Lord. I will free you from your oppression and will rescue you from your slavery in Egypt. I will redeem you with a powerful arm and great acts of judgment. 7 I will claim you as my own people, and I will be your God. Then you will know that I am the Lord your God who has freed you from your oppression in Egypt. 8 I will bring you into the land I swore to give to Abraham, Isaac, and Jacob. I will give it to you as your very own possession. I am the Lord!'"
Exodus 6:6-8 (NLT)

Slavery, I would love to say that this is a thing of the past; however, so many of my children are physically free yet enslaved in their minds and spirits. While they may not have earthly masters ordering them around and dictating their every move, they have permitted illegal masters in their flesh to control their thoughts, reactions, aspirations, pursuit of me, and overall well-being.

A few of these illegal masters are fear, addictions, past deeds, debt, people's opinions, internal clocks, etc. I want you to remember that there is still victory in the name and blood of my son, Christ Jesus. Due to the finished work of Jesus on the cross, you are able to use His name and plead His blood and command every chain and yoke of

bondage to BREAK. I AM your Deliverer. Even as I delivered the children of Israel from their bondage, I am willing and able to set you free as well. My question is, do you want to be free? Ask me for freedom and I will prove that Deliverer is still my name.

Whisper This Prayer!

God, thank you for being my strong deliverer. Thank you for being attentive to my voice and hearing my cry for deliverance. Father, I long to be free from everything that holds me in bondage. I ask that you break the chains and yokes that keep me bound. Deliver me, oh God. Help me to live a life of sustained freedom, never to return to that which you have freed me from. Help me to be diligent in protecting my gates (eyes, ears, mouth) so that I am not lured back into bondage. God, I trust you for sustained deliverance. In Jesus' name, Amen.

What things, people, systems, ways of thinking, etc. are you currently a slave to and want to break free from?

_____
_____
_____
_____
_____
_____
_____
_____
_____
_____
_____
_____
_____
_____
_____
_____
_____
_____
_____

Are you making steps to be free from these bondages or are you settled in them? What does this look like for you?

_____
_____
_____
_____
_____
_____
_____
_____
_____
_____
_____
_____

"I prayed to the Lord, and he answered me. He freed me from all my fears."

Psalm 34:4 (NLT)

DAY 12

God the Miracle Worker

29 But the people of Israel had walked through the middle of the sea on dry ground, as the water stood up like a wall on both sides. 30 That is how the Lord rescued Israel from the hand of the Egyptians that day. And the Israelites saw the bodies of the Egyptians washed up on the seashore. 31 When the people of Israel saw the mighty power that the Lord had unleashed against the Egyptians, they were filled with awe before him. They put their faith in the Lord and in his servant Moses.
Exodus 14:29-31 (NLT)

It's typically during the Christmas season that people are open to believe in miracles. Maybe it's because of the traditional holiday movies such as *Christmas Miracle, Miracle on 34th Street, A Christmas Tree Miracle*, the list goes on and on. While I delight in seeing my creation express expectation for miracles, my concern is not many people are looking to receive the miracle from ME. Whether the world believes it or not, you, my beloved, are to be confident in the fact that I am more than able to perform miracles, in any season. I AM the God of miracles. If you begin to flip through your word right now it wouldn't take you long to find a miracle. Why? Because I cut no corners when it comes to proving my love for creation. I will defy the laws of nature, that I established, to miraculously deliver my children from bondage. I will miraculously provide for widows who are on the verge of losing it all. I will hold the sun and moon in place until my people gain victory over their enemy. I will miraculously cause the blind to see, the lame to walk, the dumb to speak, and the deaf to hear. I've done it all. And guess what? I'm still in the extravagant miracle-performing business today.

There's nothing too hard for me. If you have the guts to ask, I have the power to perform. So, what miracle can I work for you today? Ask and trust me for it!

Whisper This Prayer!

God, I thank you for being a miracle worker. Thank you for your miraculous power, miraculous protection, and miraculous provision. I believe that you are still opening blinded eyes, raising the dead, supernaturally providing, and healing. You're the same God who performed miracles in the Bible days and you haven't stopped yet. Father, I am convinced that you care about me, love me, and see me. So, I ask you today to perform a miracle in my life. You know exactly where I am in need. I ask that you would do what only you can do. I believe you can. I trust you will, so I count it done. In Jesus' name, Amen.

Do you believe in miracles? Do you believe that God can and will perform a miracle for you?

_____
_____
_____
_____
_____
_____
_____
_____
_____

Can you recall a time where God performed a miracle for you?

_____
_____
_____
_____
_____
_____

_____

_____

_____

_____

_____

Activity: *Create a jar, box, or scrapbook that holds reminders of the miracles God has performed in your life. You are free to be as creative as you'd like. The purpose of this activity is to create a tangible reminder of God's faithfulness and miraculous power. When life hits hard, pull out your "miracle receipts" and remind yourself of who it is you serve.*

"O Sovereign Lord! You made the heavens and earth by your strong hand and powerful arm. Nothing is too hard for you!"

Jeremiah 32:17 (NLT)

Day 13

God Our Banner

14 After the victory, the Lord instructed Moses, "Write this down on a scroll as a permanent reminder and read it aloud to Joshua: I will erase the memory of Amalek from under heaven." 15 Moses built an altar there and named it Yahweh-Nissi (which means "the Lord is my banner"). 16 He said, "They have raised their fist against the Lord's throne, so now the Lord will be at war with Amalek generation after generation."
Exodus 17:14-16 (NLT)

Beloved, there are several guarantees in life, one of them being struggle. That may sound cruel, but it is a reality. There will be battles that you have to fight. However, do not be dismayed or frightened, because I am fighting with you and for you. Think about the children of Israel and how they were confronted by an enemy right after their triumphant trek through the Red Sea. I'm sure they saw this attack as cruel punishment, but I saw it as a chance to build warriors and to give them another reason to trust me.

It is in this battle that the Israelites (and their enemy) discover that they aren't fighting alone. Yes, they had to fight, but it was a fixed fight. All they had to do was maintain their position and trust me to give them the victory. The same is true for you, beloved. In this life, there will be opposition and full-out wars raged against you. However, you must remain mindful that the one who is with you is MIGHTY. If you allow me, I will Fight for you and I will WIN. Time after time, you will raise your banner and boast on my ability to triumph when you were powerless.

Whisper This Prayer!

God, I thank you for giving me victory time and time again. When my enemies rose up against me, you didn't leave me abandoned but you stood with me. You surrounded me with help from your sanctuary and caused me to prevail. Father, help me to trust that no matter what comes up against me today or in the future, I will NOT be defeated. I will rely on you for strategy to win every battle. You are Jehovah Nissi, the Lord my banner. You fight for me and You WIN! Therefore, I put my full trust in you. In Jesus' name, Amen.

List the battles you have faced in life that you KNOW God himself fought and won for you.

_____
_____
_____
_____
_____
_____
_____
_____
_____
_____

Are there any enemies you are facing right now? Have you inquired the Lord for your war strategy (read Exodus 17 to see Israel's winning war strategy)? If so, write it out and commit to praying it through.

_____
_____
_____
_____
_____

"What shall we say about such wonderful things as these? If God is for us, who can ever be against us?"

Romans 8:31 (NLT)

DAY 14

God the Jealous God

2 "I am the Lord your God, who rescued you from the land of Egypt, the place of your slavery. 3 "You must not have any other god but me. 4 "You must not make for yourself an idol of any kind or an image of anything in the heavens or on the earth or in the sea. 5 You must not bow down to them or worship them, for I, the Lord your God, am a jealous God who will not tolerate your affection for any other gods. I lay the sins of the parents upon their children; the entire family is affected—even children in the third and fourth generations of those who reject me. 6 But I lavish unfailing love for a thousand generations on those who love me and obey my commands…"
Exodus 20:2-6 (NLT)

How many times did you read the theme for today, just to make sure you read it correctly? I know it sounds odd to hear me, your omnipotent God, acknowledge that I am a jealous God. However, it's true. Now before you take this the wrong way, understand that my jealousy is not the same as the jealousy of mankind.

Remember, I am NOT like man (Numbers 23:19). My jealousy is nothing like the emotion you feel when your neighbor pulls up in the new black-on-black Mercedes G Wagon you've been eyeing for months. Or how you feel when your co-worker (who you know is living a raggedy life) comes into the office waving her 2-carat engagement ring from a fine, employed, God-fearing man while you're still single. Human jealousy is rooted in resentment over something another person possesses. I have a righteous jealousy for my creation. I am jealous for your full devotion. I don't want a partial or lukewarm commitment. I want you to experience all of me, while submitting all of yourself to me. Trust that I won't break your heart. I love you with a never-ending love.

Whisper This Prayer!

God, thank you for being jealous for me. Your love for me is indescribable. It goes beyond what I can comprehend with my limited understanding. Father, I repent for putting people, things, and aspirations before you. I ask that you forgive me for giving my devotion, praise, and worship to anyone but you. I vow, from this day forward, that nothing will rival against your authority and place in my life again. I will seek you first. I will Love you More. I trust you with my heart and my life. In Jesus' name, Amen.

Take inventory of your life, are there things, people, aspirations, etc., in your life that rival against God and compete for the number one spot in your life? Are you causing God to burn with jealousy?

_____

_____

_____

_____

_____

_____

_____

_____

_____

_____

_____

_____

_____

_____

_____

_____

_____

_____

Now that you've honestly identified them, how do you properly remove these "idols" from the throne of your heart? What actions do you need to take in order to place God back on the throne of your heart?

_____

_____

_____

_____

_____

_____

_____

_____

_____

"You must worship no other gods, for the Lord, whose very name is Jealous, is a God who is jealous about his relationship with you."

Exodus 34:14 (NLT))

Day 15

God Who Rewards the Fearless

23 They will never even see the land I swore to give their ancestors. None of those who have treated me with contempt will ever see it. 24 But my servant Caleb has a different attitude than the others have. He has remained loyal to me, so I will bring him into the land he explored. His descendants will possess their full share of that land.
Numbers 14:23-24 (NLT)

Well, beloved, you are halfway through your trust journey and I must say, I am proud of your intentional efforts to trust me more. You're doing well. I do, however, feel that this is the perfect day to address the pink elephant in the room, and that is your fears. How many times have you talked yourself out of a promise simply because you were afraid? No, I can't go there. No, I can't speak to them. No, I can't go back to school. My promises are indeed "yes" but it's up to you to say "amen."

Remember the twelve men that were sent to spy out the promise land, in Numbers 13. After spying out the land for 40 days and seeing firsthand the large fruit, the milk, and the honey, ten of the twelve returned with the report that the land was good BUT there are giants there. Due to their fear, these 10 men began to impart fear into the heart of every person assembled. They literally talked themselves out of their promise, all because of fear. Maybe you can relate? Thankfully, two of the spies trusted me enough to stand up and declare that they were more than able to conquer the land. Because of the faith of the two, they were permitted to enter the promise land while the ten were forbidden to enter the land they had endured so much to reach.

Which are you today? Are you one of the ten allowing what you see to chase you away from promise? Or are you one of the two boldly declaring regardless of what I see I serve a God that's greater than it all. If He said it's mine, I'm taking it! Take the focus off of your own ability and rely completely on me to lead you to victory. I will not fail you. Fear Not!

Whisper This Prayer!

God, thank you for making me as bold as a lion. Thank you for helping me to shed my fearful and timid ways and to embrace the warrior you created me to be. Help me not to back down when difficulties arise. Help me to be constantly aware of the fact that you are with me. If you are with me, I cannot fail. I trust you, therefore I have no reason to fear. In Jesus' name, Amen.

Have you ever had God give you an assignment that made you feel small or inadequate?

_____
_____
_____
_____
_____
_____
_____
_____
_____
_____
_____
_____

How did you (or will you) fight these feelings in order to press on to receive the promise of God?

_____
_____
_____
_____

"The wicked run away when no one is chasing them, but the godly are as bold as lions."

Proverbs 28:1 (NLT)

Day 16

God the Defender

20 Listen, I received a command to bless; God has blessed, and I cannot reverse it! 21 No misfortune is in his plan for Jacob; no trouble is in store for Israel. For the Lord their God is with them; he has been proclaimed their king. 22 God brought them out of Egypt; for them he is as strong as a wild ox. 23 No curse can touch Jacob; no magic has any power against Israel. For now, it will be said of Jacob, 'What wonders God has done for Israel!'
Numbers 23:20-23 (NLT)

When you think of the word defender your mind more than likely goes to some type of athletic event. You imagine a defensive lineman on a football field or a basketball player on defense on the court. In both instances there is one person or a group of people protecting the ball from being stolen or protecting their teammates from unseen attacks by the opposing team.

In the same way that a point guard or a linebacker defends, I want to remind you that I Am the God that is always on post, defending you from incoming attacks of the enemy. I Am your Great Defender. I continually protect you from car collisions, unforeseen accidents, and robbers. Beyond the natural, I protect you from spiritual missiles launched from hell, intended to destroy your sanity, your ministry, your marriage, and your life. When you are

alert and even when you are completely oblivious, I am there to protect and cover you. Trust me.

Whisper This Prayer!

God, thank you for being my great defender. Thank you for protecting me from dangers seen and unseen. Thank you for lifting up a standard against the enemy every time he seeks to come in like a flood. Father, I ask that you would help me to be more aware of my surroundings in the natural and in the spirit. Allow nothing to come upon me unaware. Teach me to be alert and attentive to your promptings. I trust you to take good care of me. In Jesus' name, Amen.

Can you think of an instance where you know God intercepted the enemy's plans to steal, kill, and destroy, on your behalf?

_____
_____
_____
_____
_____
_____
_____
_____
_____
_____
_____
_____
_____

"This I declare about the Lord: He alone is my refuge, my place of safety; he is my God, and I trust him."

Psalm 91:2 (NLT)

Day 17

God the Cycle Breaker

1 Then we turned, and took our journey into the wilderness by the way of the Red sea, as the Lord spake unto me: and we compassed mount Seir many days. 2 And the Lord spake unto me, saying, 3 Ye have compassed this mountain long enough: turn you northward.
Deuteronomy 2:1-3 (KJV)

Cycles, a series of events that are regularly completed in the same order. Have you found yourself going around the same mountains over and over again? You experience moments of great victory and freedom but at the same time every year, you find yourself reverting back to your regularly scheduled program.

You finally broke free from bum #1 and here you are six months later with bum #2. You worked so hard to pay off your credit cards, but here you are 12 months later with two new maxed out credit cards. No condemnation, stop beating yourself up, you're just in a cycle. Now that you've identified it, bring it to me and I'll break it, but you must then listen for my instructions. For it is not enough for you to just hear me say, "turn northward," you must be in agreement and make the physical adjustments necessary to head in a new direction. In order to remain free from the cycle, I need you to commit to prayer, discipline, intentionality, identify your triggers, and close every necessary door. Yes, this process requires your effort, but know that it's worth it. You've spent enough time here. Today, hear me crying out, "turn northward."

Whisper This Prayer!

God, thank you for breaking every unhealthy cycle in my life. Thank you for bringing to my attention the things, thoughts, actions, people, and habits that I continue to go back to after you have freed me. Today, Father, I ask for your strength as I commit to living free of every cycle that once entangled me. Help me to make the right choices and to seek you in all I do. I'm no longer satisfied with momentary freedom, I want to LIVE FREE, permanently. Only with you is this possible, so I trust you to carry me through. In Jesus' name, Amen.

Can you identify an unhealthy cycle you need to break free from?

_____
_____
_____
_____
_____
_____
_____
_____
_____

Can you connect this cycle with a particular life event, time of year, interaction, person? (Really think about it! Let's find the door to close. What's the common denominator found in every cycle reset?)

_____
_____
_____
_____
_____
_____

God has the power to break the cycle, but what are you going to do to remain cycle free? What actions will you commit to? What boundaries are you putting in place?

_____
_____
_____
_____
_____
_____
_____
_____
_____
_____
_____

"So Christ has truly set us free. Now make sure that you stay free, and don't get tied up again in slavery to the law."

Galatians 5:1 (NLT)

Day 18

God of the Encore

> *21 Then Joshua said to the Israelites, "In the future your children will ask, 'What do these stones mean?' 22 Then you can tell them, 'This is where the Israelites crossed the Jordan on dry ground.' 23 For the Lord your God dried up the river right before your eyes, and he kept it dry until you were all across, just as he did at the Red Sea when he dried it up until we had all crossed over. 24 He did this so all the nations of the earth might know that the Lord's hand is powerful, and so you might fear the Lord your God forever."*
> **Joshua 4:21-24 (NLT)**

If I did it before, I can do it again. Unlike many of your favorite singers, I'm not a one-hit wonder. Over the course of time I have proven that if I accomplish something once, I can surely do it again. Remember the children of Israel and how I displayed my power at the Red Sea, breathing on the deep waters, causing it to part so that they could walk on dry ground to the other side. Here they are again at the edge of a body of water, this time the Jordan River, needing to get across. Why not give an encore! While my methodology changed, the result was the same. I held up the flow of water and allowed them to cross on dry ground. Here's what I want you to remember, beloved, I may switch up my

method but the outcome will always be a Miracle! Whether you have personally seen a miracle or heard the testimony of a miracle that I've worked, know that I am able to do it again. Don't look for it to happen the same way, just look for the same outcome. This is a good place to lift your hands and cry out, "ENCORE LORD…ENCORE."

Whisper This Prayer!

God, I thank you for being the God of the encore. You are the God who can DO IT AGAIN! You're the God of repeat miracles. I bless you today because while your method may change, the outcome remains the same. You always get the Glory! Today, I ask in faith for an encore performance in my life. You've healed before, God, heal again. You've provided before, Father, provide again. You've opened doors for me before, Lord, so I know you can do it again. I need an encore. You're the same God, for you cannot change. Your blood still has power. Your name is still the most powerful name. You are still God. You're still in control. I trust that you can do it again. I wait on you. In Jesus' name, Amen.

Make a list of all of the wonderful things God has done for you. Go back as far as you can remember. Remind yourself of the faithfulness of God towards you.

_____
_____
_____
_____
_____
_____
_____
_____
_____
_____
_____
_____
_____
_____
_____
_____
_____
_____
_____
_____
_____

What is it that you need God to do again in your life?

_____
_____
_____
_____
_____
_____
_____
_____
_____
_____
_____
_____
_____
_____
_____
_____

"Restore our fortunes, Lord, as streams renew the desert."

Psalm 126:4 (NLT)

Day 19

God the Strategist

2 And the Lord said to Joshua: "See! I have given Jericho into your hand, its king, and the mighty men of valor. 3 You shall march around the city, all you men of war; you shall go all around the city once. This you shall do six days. 4 And seven priests shall bear seven trumpets of rams' horns before the ark. But the seventh day you shall march around the city seven times, and the priests shall blow the trumpets. 5 It shall come to pass, when they make a long blast with the ram's horn, and when you hear the sound of the trumpet, that all the people shall shout with a great shout; then the wall of the city will fall down flat. And the people shall go up every man straight before him."
Joshua 6:2-5 (NKJV)

In life you will face moments that make you feel unqualified, incapable, and just plain small. There will be times when I bring you face to face with giant obstacles that make you chuckle and say, "Really God." Instead of shrinking back and telling me what you can't do, I urge you to seek me for Strategy. Know that if I bring you to a mountain, surely I have a PLAN for how I'm going to get you over it. Fear NOT. Seek me and listen for my instructions. I may not give you the full plan, but I will give you enough to get started. Commit to walking out the instructions given and I will show you the rest as you go. Remember my servant Abraham in Genesis 12 and how I didn't give him any instructions outside of "leave your native country and your family and go to a land that I WILL show you." Just as he had questions in His heart but chose to trust my voice and my unspoken plan, I need you to do the same. Trust me enough to obey me, even in the absence of details. Obey my commands and take the first step, for the full strategy is sure to follow. I will not fail you.

Whisper This Prayer!

God, I thank you for being the master strategist. Thank you for sharing your knowledge and wisdom with me. Today, Father, I seek you for strategy that I might carry out the plans you have for my life. I acknowledge that I don't know it all. You are my only help. Speak to my heart. Give me your direction, even if it's one step at a time. Help me to truly rest in you. I trust you to get me to my destination safely and on time. In Jesus' name, Amen.

What strategy (plan) has God given you that you have completely ignored? (This can relate to business, relationships, schooling, motherhood, etc.)

What portion of the strategies given to you by God have you put to work? Is it possible for you to press harder into these areas?

_____
_____
_____
_____
_____
_____
_____
_____
_____
_____
_____
_____
_____
_____
_____

"We can make our plans, but the Lord determines our steps."

Proverbs 16:9 (NLT)

DAY 20

God of the Impossible

> 12 On the day the Lord gave the Israelites victory over the Amorites, Joshua prayed to the Lord in front of all the people of Israel. He said, "Let the sun stand still over Gibeon, and the moon over the valley of Aijalon." 13 So the sun stood still and the moon stayed in place until the nation of Israel had defeated its enemies. Is this event not recorded in The Book of Jashar? The sun stayed in the middle of the sky, and it did not set as on a normal day. 14 There has never been a day like this one before or since, when the Lord answered such a prayer. Surely the Lord fought for Israel that day!
> **Joshua 10:12-14 (NLT)**

I want you to believe me for the impossible. If you're honest, you've been praying small. You have learned to trust me for bill money and parking spaces at the mall, which I appreciate, but I want to pull you from the shallow end of trust into the deep. Joshua was so confident in my ability to be God and to do the impossible that he asked me to make the sun and moon stand still. He asked me to do something he had never seen done before. Something that had never been done in history. I desire for you to walk in and pray with the same confidence. Ask me for the hard thing. Yes, the thing that you have been fighting not to mention to me in prayer. The thing you've been too afraid to even say aloud. Ask me to make you a miracle. Ask me to chase the cancer out of your body. Ask me to give you the one idea that will change your entire life and legacy. Ask me to fill your womb with a child after the doctors said you have a 0% chance of conceiving. Ask me. Pray that BIG prayer. I've said it before and I'll say it again, if you have the guts to ask, I have the power to perform. Trust me for it, beloved. ASK!

Whisper This Prayer!

God, I thank you for being the God of the impossible. Thank you for reminding me that there is nothing too hard for you. There is no battle that your arms are too short to fight. Today I make my heart believe you for the impossible. You are able to heal the incurable disease, to save the unreachable child, and to redeem the time that has been wasted. You can do it. I believe you. My trust is in you. In Jesus' name, Amen.

Is there an impossibility in your life that you have been almost fearful to present to God? What is it?

Can you take a moment to write down all the impossibilities that God has already made possible for you. (Example, you thought you'd never get to go to college. You were told it was impossible for you to be accepted, get funding, etc. Yet here you are with a degree. Some of you with more than one. He made your impossibility possible.)

_____

_____

_____

_____

_____

_____

_____

_____

_____

_____

_____

"He replied, "What is impossible for people is possible with God."

Luke 18:27 (NLT)

DAY 21

God Our Peace

22 Now Gideon perceived that He was the Angel of the Lord. So Gideon said, "Alas, O Lord God! For I have seen the Angel of the Lord face to face. 23 Then the Lord said to him, "Peace be with you; do not fear, you shall not die." 24 So Gideon built an altar there to the Lord, and called it The-Lord-Is-Peace. To this day it is still in Ophrah of the Abiezrites.
Judges 6:22-24 (NKJV)

Life can get so loud and consuming at times, can't it? I see you working hard to manage family issues, children, faith, finances, career/business, school, ministry, and difficult people. I know it can be a lot and you often feel as if you're being swallowed by the waves of life. I see you. Lift your head out of the water and hear my voice calling to you, "choose peace, my beloved." I extend my hand and invite you to grab ahold of it today, even as I did for my servant Peter who went from walking on the water to sinking in it.

Don't be overwhelmed by the winds and the waves, I Am here with you. Use your tools. Grab your head phones, pull up your worship playlist and sing until you've drowned out the noise of your environment. When the bills are piling up and you feel like you're drowning in debt, grab a scripture like Philippians 4:19, "and my God shall supply all of my needs according to His riches…" and quote it until my peace overtakes you. When your body isn't functioning properly, lay hands on yourself and decree healing and wholeness until my peace overrides the pain. Choose not to worry or fear, but choose Peace. Take your eyes off of the situation and find a way to fix them on me, your Hope! My peace I give to you today.

Whisper This Prayer!

God, I thank you for your peace, that truly goes beyond understanding. Thank you, Lord, for allowing me to find shelter and refuge in you. When life gets crazy and my fears seek to overtake me, you rush in with your peace that soothes my doubts and calms my fears. Today, Father, I ask that you will help me to intentionally seek peace. That I won't sit in chaotic atmospheres waiting for them to change themselves but I will take an active role and invoke your peace in my space. I take rest in you today, Lord, for you are my peace. In Jesus' name, Amen.

During the chaotic and stressful moments of life, what/who do you rely on for Peace?

_____
_____
_____
_____
_____
_____
_____
_____

Have you truly learned how to embrace the reality of God's peace?

_____
_____
_____
_____
_____
_____
_____
_____
_____

What are some practical activities you feel God leading you to implement in your life, to invoke His peace? (i.e., meditating on scripture, playing soothing worship music, reciting a particular Bible verse, etc.)

_____
_____
_____
_____
_____
_____
_____
_____
_____
_____
_____
_____
_____

"In peace I will lie down and sleep, for you alone, O Lord, will keep me safe."

Psalm 4:8 (NLT)

Day 22

God the Restorer

28 Then Samson prayed to the Lord, "Sovereign Lord, remember me again. O God, please strengthen me just one more time. With one blow let me pay back the Philistines for the loss of my two eyes." 29 Then Samson put his hands on the two center pillars that held up the temple. Pushing against them with both hands, 30 he prayed, "Let me die with the Philistines." And the temple crashed down on the Philistine rulers and all the people. So he killed more people when he died than he had during his entire lifetime.
Judges 16:28-30 (NLT)

Is there any feeling more frustrating than looking for something and it not being where it should be? You know you put your debit card in your wallet after your last purchase, but you've searched in every crack and crevice and it's not there. Then it hits you, "I've lost it." Immediately, you get that sinking feeling in the bottom of your belly. Beloved, I feel your pain. While it is easy for the bank to restore that debit card, there are some things that you lose that aren't easy to replace.

Things like time, joy, peace, love, and passion. These things can only be replaced through my restoring power. Be reminded that I Am the God that restores. I can give you back what you've lost. I can make up for the time you've wasted. I can replenish the money you've squandered. I can restore the love, joy, and self-esteem that counterfeit love robbed you of. Yes, this is an easy thing for me. Even as I returned strength to Samson's weakened body at his request, I can restore your strength today. You need only to trust and ask me.

Whisper This Prayer!

God, I thank you for the power of restoration. Thank you for restoring every good thing that I've lost and the good things that were stolen from me over the years. Father, I repent for the part I played in the loss of certain things in my life. The people I pushed away, the opportunities I squandered, the money and time I wasted, and the things I took for granted. Forgive me, Lord. Today, Father, I take you at your word and I decree that I am being restored. You are restoring my joy, my peace, my health, lost time, passion, and zeal for the things of God. You are restoring my family, my marriage, my ministry, my money, and my strength. Thank you for what you're doing in me. I trust you, Lord, for complete restoration. In Jesus' name, Amen.

What things, possessions, positions, relationships, dreams, etc., have you lost that you know you were meant to possess? List them out and ask the Lord to restore.

_____
_____
_____
_____
_____
_____
_____
_____
_____

"In his kindness God called you to share in his eternal glory by means of Christ Jesus. So after you have suffered a little while, he will restore, support, and strengthen you, and he will place you on a firm foundation."

1 Peter 5:10 (NLT)

DAY 23

God the Void Filler

> 3 Then Elimelech died, and Naomi was left with her two sons. 4 The two sons married Moabite women. One married a woman named Orpah, and the other a woman named Ruth. But about ten years later, 5 both Mahlon and Kilion died. This left Naomi alone, without her two sons or her husband.
> **Ruth 1:3-5 (NLT)**

Yesterday you leaned into trusting me to restore the things that you have lost. While I delight in restoring, I must share that there are a small number of things that I can't give back, one being your loved ones that have come to join me in heaven. I know it pains you to even remember that they are no longer present with you in the natural, but I had to bring this up to remind you that I am the void filler.

Remember my servant Naomi, who had not only lost her husband but also her two sons, her protection, her provision, and her family's legacy. Fortunately for Naomi, both of her sons were married to Moabite women who Loved her as their own mother. Naomi didn't desire for them to live bitter, unmarried lives, so she encouraged them to go back home to their families and start new lives. While one of the daughters, Orpah, took Naomi up on the offer, Ruth declined. Ruth gives Naomi the comfort of knowing that wherever she went,

Ruth would be right there with her. Ruth knew the type of sacrifice this would be for her, but being with and caring for her mother-in-law meant more. In that moment, Ruth filled a void in the heart of Naomi that was left by the loss of her husband and sons. In that moment, Naomi could be certain that she wasn't without love or care. In the same way, hear me calling out to you saying, you may have lost people that you loved dearly, but you aren't left desolate.

Even in the midst of sadness I am bringing you reason to smile. Look around you. For just a moment, choose to not focus all of your attention on what's missing but on what remains. I am here to fill every void and empty space. Don't push my provision away, but instead, receive it with an open heart. This is my gift to you. Take heart, there's more where this came from.

Whisper This Prayer!

Father God, I thank you for being the God that fills every void in my life. Thank you for filling my heart and my life with good things. Forgive me Lord for giving so much attention to the things I lost that I overlooked the blessings you had already provided for me. Father, teach me to treasure what remains. Teach me to honor the relationships, friendships, provisions, and love that I have. I am not alone and I am not abandoned, for you are with me. In Jesus' name, Amen.

Are there any people (or things) in your life that you are currently grieving the loss of?

_____
_____
_____
_____
_____
_____
_____
_____
_____
_____
_____
_____
_____

While the absence of this person (or thing) is real, are you able to see what God has sent you to fill the void? List these void fillers and celebrate them.

_____
_____
_____

"Our hearts ache, but we always have joy. We are poor, but we give spiritual riches to others. We own nothing, and yet we have everything."

2 Corinthians 6:10 (NLT)

DAY 24

The God Who Rewards Sacrifice

10 Ruth fell at his feet and thanked him warmly. "What have I done to deserve such kindness?" she asked. "I am only a foreigner." 11 "Yes, I know," Boaz replied. "But I also know about everything you have done for your mother-in-law since the death of your husband. I have heard how you left your father and mother and your own land to live here among complete strangers. 12 May the Lord, the God of Israel, under whose wings you have come to take refuge, reward you fully for what you have done."
Ruth 2:10-12 (NLT)

Over the years, religion has painted me to be a harsh God, lacking mercy and care for humanity. This is far from the truth. I am a loving God and Father. And even as a natural father rewards his child for performing well in school or putting forth their best efforts on the field, I, too, reward my children for their genuine service, heartfelt effort, and achievements. I do not tell you this to persuade you to do what is right, for that should be your heart's desire even if there is no recognition. I say this to let you know that my eyes are always on you. I'm not just looking at your actions but the heart behind the actions, and I'm taking record. Yes, I will not forget. I will not forget how hard you have worked for me and how you have shown your love to me by caring for other believers. I will reward you. The things that you did in secret to be a blessing to others, the money you gave that you needed for yourself, the encouragement you gave when you needed encouragement yourself, I saw it, and I will reward you openly.

Whisper This Prayer!

Father God, I thank you for being the God that rewards me. You aren't a God that's only concerned with chastising me for my shortcomings, but you're a God that delights in rewarding me for the good things I do. I pray, Father, that you will align me with those that you have established to hand deliver your rewards to me. Thank you for being a good father who sees me and celebrates me. I love you with my whole heart. In Jesus' name, Amen.

Can you recall a time where God brought undeniable favor into your life and immediately brought back to your mind a moment or season of sacrifice?

_____
_____
_____
_____
_____
_____
_____
_____
_____
_____
_____
_____
_____
_____
_____
_____
_____
_____
_____
_____

Make a list of your personal sacrifices of this season and remind yourself that each one is worth it.

_____
_____
_____
_____
_____
_____
_____
_____
_____
_____
_____
_____
_____

"Give your gifts in private, and your Father, who sees everything, will reward you."

Matthew 6:4 (NLT)

DAY 25

The God Who Favors

15 When Ruth went back to work again, Boaz ordered his young men, "Let her gather grain right among the sheaves without stopping her. 16 And pull out some heads of barley from the bundles and drop them on purpose for her. Let her pick them up, and don't give her a hard time!" 17 So Ruth gathered barley there all day, and when she beat out the grain that evening, it filled an entire basket.
Ruth 2:15-17 (NLT)

I Am the God that favors you. I delight in showing kindness to you beyond what you feel is due or usual. Many say that my favor isn't fair. I say that favor is only unfair to the person who refuses to receive it for themselves. I don't play favorites. What I give to one of my children I will gladly give to all. For no good thing will I withhold for them that walk upright before me. Not only will I favor you, but I will cause others to favor you as well.

    Don't be alarmed when people take a liking to you. Let down your natural wall and receive what I am releasing to you. Pressed down, shaken together, and running over shall I cause men to give unto your bosom. I can and will use anyone to get my blessings to you. For Ruth, I used Boaz, for you, I will use a boss, a co-worker, a fellow church member, or even a perfect stranger waiting in the line of a store. Yes, I will cause prefect strangers to look upon you with favor to make the impossible possible and turn your lack into abundance. There's nothing too hard for me. There are no limits to my love for you. Receive my favor!

Whisper This Prayer!

Father God, I thank you for the great favor you have lavished upon my life. Thank you for giving me what I could never earn or even deserve based on my own merit. Thank you for using the kindness of perfect strangers to remind me of your great care for me. Thank you for placing my name and my concerns on the hearts of others. Thank you for making ways for me when I could see no way. You are indeed worthy of my trust. In Jesus' name, Amen.

Where in your life is it evident that the favor of God is upon you?

_____
_____
_____
_____
_____
_____
_____
_____
_____
_____
_____
_____
_____
_____
_____
_____
_____
_____
_____
_____
_____

Similar to Ruth, in what ways has God allowed others to favor you? Maybe it was a position you didn't apply for, a line of credit you didn't qualify for, or the blossoming of a relationship that you had convinced yourself you weren't worthy of.

_____
_____
_____
_____
_____
_____
_____
_____
_____
_____

"And may the Lord our God show us his approval and make our efforts successful. Yes, make our efforts successful!"

Psalm 90:17 (NLT)

DAY 26

God That Gives Beauty for Ashes

> 14 Then the women of the town said to Naomi, "Praise the Lord, who has now provided a redeemer for your family! May this child be famous in Israel. 15 May he restore your youth and care for you in your old age. For he is the son of your daughter-in-law who loves you and has been better to you than seven sons!" 16 Naomi took the baby and cuddled him to her breast. And she cared for him as if he were her own. 17 The neighbor women said, "Now at last Naomi has a son again!" And they named him Obed. He became the father of Jesse and the grandfather of David.
> **Ruth 4:14-17 (NLT)**

There is no sorrow that I cannot turn to gladness. There is no tear that I can't turn to laughter. There is no pain that I can't bring power of out. I am the God of transformation and divine turnarounds. I am the God of your dark days just as I am the God of your days of victory. I am there in the midst of it all working it all together for you. While you may not see it today, I have great plans for your pain. For yes, if I allowed it, it's because I plan to make use of it. For how could you testify of my healing power if you never needed it? How could you testify of my delivering power if you were never bound? How could you confidently tell the world that I give beauty for ashes if you didn't walk the scorched ground of disappointment? Trust me when I say, something good is coming out of this ugly situation. Remember my servant Naomi and how I gave her the love of seven sons through one devoted daughter-in-law. How I breathed life into her deceased legacy by giving her a grandson who would initiate the linage through which I would send my own son, Jesus. I make all things beautiful in my time. Endure, my beloved.

Whisper This Prayer!

Father God, I thank you for making all things beautiful in my life. Thank you for causing the hardships of my life to produce power within me. Help me to trust you to transform the darkness I am in today into something you get glory from. Help me to understand that you aren't punishing me. You're pruning me. You're building me up. You are making every area of my life beautiful. I now believe that. In Jesus' name, Amen.

In what areas of your life are you witnessing the transformative power of God?

_____
_____
_____
_____
_____
_____
_____
_____
_____
_____
_____
_____

Write down the aspects of your life that you desire God to completely transform. Have a conversation with God about these things and trust Him to make it beautiful, in His perfect time.

_____
_____
_____
_____

"To all who mourn in Israel, he will give a crown of beauty for ashes, a joyous blessing instead of mourning, festive praise instead of despair. In their righteousness, they will be like great oaks that the Lord has planted for his own glory."

Isaiah 61:3 (NLT)

DAY 27

The God That Remembers

16 Don't think I am a wicked woman! For I have been praying out of great anguish and sorrow." 17 "In that case," Eli said, "go in peace! May the God of Israel grant the request you have asked of him." 18 "Oh, thank you, sir!" she exclaimed. Then she went back and began to eat again, and she was no longer sad. 19 The entire family got up early the next morning and went to worship the Lord once more. Then they returned home to Ramah. When Elkanah slept with Hannah, the Lord remembered her plea, 20 and in due time she gave birth to a son. She named him Samuel, for she said, "I asked the Lord for him."
1 Samuel 1:16-20 (NLT)

Memory, a gift that many take for granted in their youth but treasure in their latter days. As you grow older you will find yourself struggling at times to remember birth dates, pin numbers, passwords, and even the names of your own children. Contrary to your dimming memory, I want to remind you that my memory never weakens. I remember every promise I've made. I remember every word I've spoken. I remember the prayers you prayed and the tears you cried. I remember your name, your needs, and your deeds. I haven't missed a thing, neither have I forgotten.

My promises are still yes and amen. Trust that I will bring every promise to pass, at the

preordained time. I have not forgotten you, my beloved.

Whisper This Prayer!

Father God, I thank you for being the God that remembers. You are the God who hears our prayers and responds to us in your perfect timing. I give you glory today because I know that you have not forgotten me nor the prayers I have lifted up to you. Father, you keep good records; therefore, I stand boldly before you knowing that in due season I shall reap if I faint not. Help me, Father, to remain strong during this waiting period. Don't allow my faith to waver. Teach me how to recall and remember your goodness until you REMEMBER ME. In Jesus' name, Amen.

Do you have any prayer requests that you have laid before God that you feel He's overlooked or forgotten? Write them down and then take them before the Lord again. Intentionally reengage your faith and expectation for the manifestation of these requests.

_____
_____
_____
_____
_____
_____
_____
_____
_____
_____
_____
_____
_____

"Remember me, Lord, when you show favor to your people; come near and rescue me."

Psalm 106:4 (NLT)

The God That Reveals the Future

11 Then the Lord said to Samuel, "I am about to do a shocking thing in Israel. 12 I am going to carry out all my threats against Eli and his family, from beginning to end. 13 I have warned him that judgment is coming upon his family forever, because his sons are blaspheming God and he hasn't disciplined them. 14 So I have vowed that the sins of Eli and his sons will never be forgiven by sacrifices or offerings."
1 Samuel 3:11-14 (NLT)

Privy to the past, present, and future, I Am the Omniscient God. I have full awareness and infinite knowledge of all that exists in and out of time. I know it all. Nothing catches me by surprise. One thing I am not is a hoarder of my vast knowledge. I am always seeking out hearts that I can share my secrets with, in order to accomplish my will in the Earth.

    At any given moment, whether prompted by your petition or simply because I trust you, I will reveal things to you that have not yet manifested in the Earth. There are times that I share information with you so that you can share with others to renew their hope for the future and desire to live. At times I will share secret information so that you can warn of impending dangers. I share to ensure that my will is being prayed and worked in the Earth. Call out to me and I will answer you and tell you great and unsearchable things that you have not known. I trust you!

Whisper This Prayer!

Father God, I thank you for being the God that reveals the things that are to come to your servants. Teach us how to steward these words. I ask that you would show me what I am to do with these mysteries. Teach me when to share and when to keep quiet. When I am to pray and when I am to act. May I always be found as a trustworthy keeper of your secrets. In Jesus' name, Amen.

Reflect back on promises you have received from God, whether through a dream or a prophet, related to your future, and record them below. (You may have to ask the Lord to remind you of them if it's been a while.)

_____
_____
_____
_____
_____
_____
_____
_____
_____
_____
_____
_____
_____
_____
_____
_____
_____
_____

Of the promises that were brought to your remembrance, record that which has come to pass. Rejoice over the things God has already done!

_____
_____
_____
_____
_____
_____
_____
_____
_____
_____
_____
_____
_____
_____

"Ask me and I will tell you remarkable secrets you do not know about things to come."

Jeremiah 33:3 (NLT)

God Our Strength

28 Have you never heard? Have you never understood The Lord is the everlasting God, the Creator of all the earth. He never grows weak or weary. No one can measure the depths of his understanding. 29 He gives power to the weak and strength to the powerless. 30 Even youths will become weak and tired, and young men will fall in exhaustion. 31 But those who trust in the Lord will find new strength. They will soar high on wings like eagles. They will run and not grow weary. They will walk and not faint.
Isaiah 40:28-31 (NLT)

Well, my beloved, we are almost to the end of the journey. Look how far you've come. Look at how much you've learned about me. I know that eventually the "high" of this journey will begin to fade and you may even struggle to remember the characteristics you've learned. There are two things that I want you to be confident of, the first being, I Am your strength. On the days that you have to fight to get out of bed, the moments when the weight of the world is too heavy to bear, and when you are just plain OVER IT...ALL OF IT, I want you to remember that your strength isn't enough.

Regardless of how powerful and anointed you are, how many devils you cast out, how much money you have, how many businesses you own, how many sermons you preach or songs you lead, at the end of the day, you are still human. All of humanity is in need of my strength. Therefore, I have created a place where you can run and find my strength. In this place there's peace, joy, reassurance, guidance, clarity, and so much more.

This place is my presence. You are at any time permitted to request access to this secret place. Because I care for you, I welcome you to cast all of your cares at my feet. I invite you to exchange your sorrow for my joy and your heaviness for praise. You don't have to carry that heavy load on your own. I am here to be your strength.

Whisper This Prayer!

God, thank you for being my strength. In my weakest moments you have taught me to cast my cares upon you because you care for me. Today, Father, I repent for carrying loads that you have asked me to give to you. I acknowledge that I am not a superhero. I make the conscious decision to lay down every weight I've been carrying and to trust you to take good care of me. Thank you for being with me. Thank you for being my help. Thank you for being my strength. In Jesus' name, Amen.

In what area of life do you need the strength of God most?

Honest reflection, in your moments of weakness, is God the first person you turn to?

_____
_____
_____
_____
_____
_____
_____
_____

Have you learned how to properly off-load your worries and cares onto God? Or are you carrying around loads that God is asking you to exchange? What do you need to hand over to Him today?

_____
_____
_____
_____
_____
_____
_____
_____

"See, God has come to save me. I will trust in him and not be afraid. The Lord God is my strength and my song; he has given me victory."

Isaiah 12:2 (NLT)

DAY 30

God is Love

3 Long ago the Lord said to Israel: "I have loved you, my people, with an everlasting love. With unfailing love I have drawn you to myself."
Jeremiah 31:3 (NLT)

As I mentioned yesterday, as we bring this journey to a close, there are two things that I want you to have unshakeable confidence in. The first is that I Am your strength. But most importantly, I need you to be resolved, settled in, and convinced that I LOVE YOU. If you ever find it hard to trust any of my characteristics, please don't allow anything to shake your confidence in the truth of my great Love for you. When you're having a hard time trusting that I will provide for you, remember my love for you. When it's tough to trust that I am with you, remember my love for you. When you're battling sickness, remember my love for you.

Through it all, allow MY LOVE to chase away your fears. You can trust me because I love you. I don't love you with a carnal, temporary love as the world does. I love you with an everlasting, eternal love. Receive my love today. YOU ARE MY BELOVED!

Whisper This Prayer!

Father God, I thank you for being the God that consistently loves me. When I'm right, you love me. When I'm wrong, you still love me. When I'm up and when I'm down, your love remains. Thank you for not permitting anything to separate me from your great love. As a way to show my gratitude, my heart's desire is to love you back fully. I surrender my heart to you. Pour your love into me and receive the offering of my love back to you. In Jesus' name, Amen.

Take a moment to reflect on the unchanging love of God that has been shown to you over the course of your life. From your heart, write God a letter of gratitude for His love (feel free to grab a notebook for more writing space). After you've completed this letter commit to referring back to it when troubles rise or when you need a reminder of how loved you are.

_____
_____
_____
_____
_____
_____
_____
_____
_____
_____
_____
_____
_____
_____
_____
_____
_____
_____
_____
_____

"Such love has no fear because perfect love expels all fear. If we are afraid, it is for fear of punishment, and this shows that we have not fully experienced his perfect love. We love each other because he loved us first."

1 John 4:18-19 (NLT)

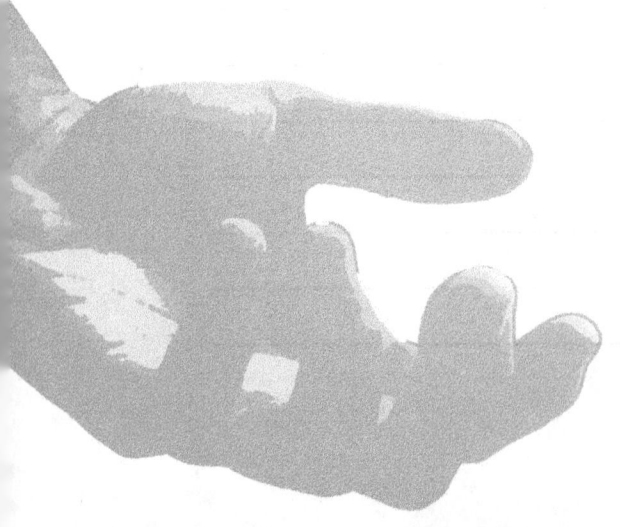

www.ingramcontent.com/pod-product-compliance
Lightning Source LLC
Chambersburg PA
CBHW070503100426
42743CB00010B/1744